Contents

All kinds of animals

There are many kinds of animals.

An ant is a tiny animal. You need a magnifying glass to see it well.

An elephant is a huge animal. This one is more than twice as tall as Tom.

Some animals have wings and can fly.

Some animals have fins and can swim.

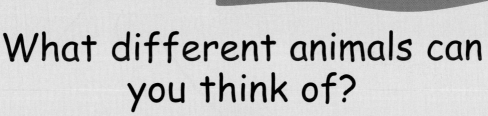

Most animals have legs and can walk, jump and run.

What different animals can you think of?

Insects

Animals that have wings and six legs are called insects.

This moth has large wings.

A beetle's wings are on its back. They are difficult to see.

A ladybird is a beetle. You can only see its wings when it flies.

Insects hatch from eggs. The young that hatch out don't always look like their parents.

Butterflies are insects that begin life as caterpillars.

Is this animal an insect? Turn the page to find out.

Is it an insect?

It's a spider. A spider is not an insect because it has eight legs and no wings.

Here are some animals. Which ones are insects?

A. Fly

B. Grasshopper

C. Woodlice

D. Dragonfly

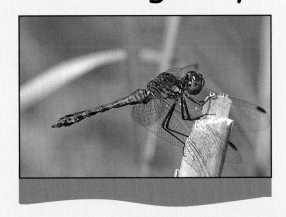

E. Millipede

F. Earthworm

G. Slug

H. Beetle

Soft body, no legs

Earthworms, slugs and snails have long soft bodies and no legs.

An earthworm has rings of muscles along its body.

A slug has a thicker body and feelers on its head. It has a hole in its side to help it breathe.

A snail has a body like a slug. You can tell it is a snail because it has a shell too.

Which of these are earthworms, slugs and snails?

A

B

C

D

There are many different kinds of earthworm. Some kinds of earthworms can be very long.

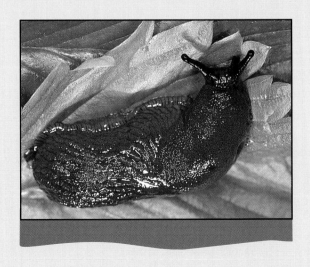

Slugs can be red, black or yellow as well as brown.

There are different kinds of snail. These two types live in water.

The pond snail has a twisted shell.

The ramshorn snail has a coiled shell.

What other animals do you know that live in water? Turn the page to find one type.

Fish

Fish live in water.

Fish are covered in scales.

When a fish swims it moves its body from side to side.

Fish use their fins to steer through the water.

A fish has gills on its head.

Gills let fish breathe underwater. They cannot breathe out of water.

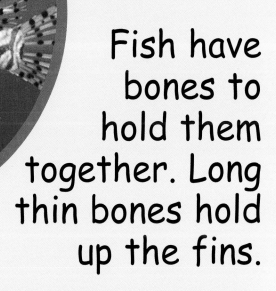

Fish have bones to hold them together. Long thin bones hold up the fins.

Amphibians

Some animals begin their life in water and later live on land. They are called amphibians.

The tadpole looks like a fish and lives in water.

It grows and changes into a frog.

Frogs live on land. They have skin covered in slime.

Toads look like frogs but they usually have warty skin.

A newt is an amphibian with a broad flat tail.

What animal looks like a newt but only lives on land? Turn the page to find out.

Reptiles

Lizards look like newts. Lizards live on land and are reptiles.

The tortoise is a reptile with a shell. It has scales on its head, legs and tail. All reptiles have scales on their body.

Some reptiles, like this snake, have no legs.

Turtles are reptiles that live in water. They don't have gills to breathe like fish. They swim to the surface to breathe.

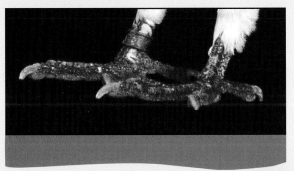

This animal has got scales on its feet. Is it a reptile? Turn the page to find out.

Birds

The animal is a bird.

It has got a beak.

It is covered in feathers.

It has got wings.

It has two legs covered in scales.

Birds use their wings to fly.

Some birds cannot fly. Their wings are too small to fly. The ostrich is a bird that cannot fly.

There are lots of different birds. How many can you think of?

23

Mammals

Animals with hair are called mammals.

A rabbit is covered in hair, called fur.

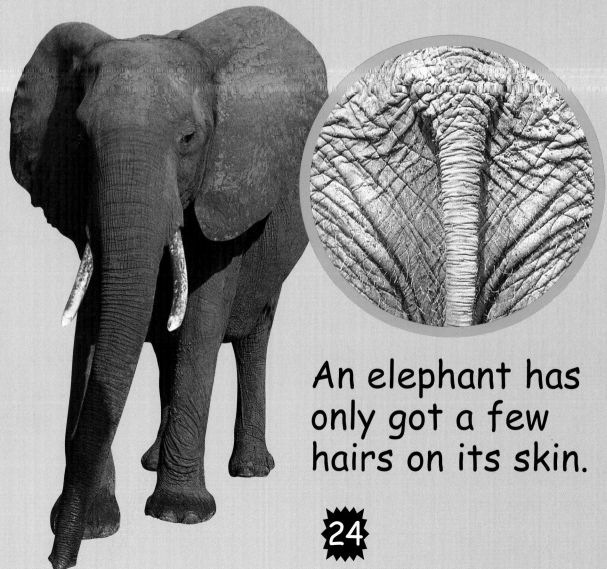

An elephant has only got a few hairs on its skin.

Most mammals live on land but some live in water.

Dolphins are mammals that live in the sea. Sea mammals go to the surface of the water to breathe.

Bats are mammals that can fly.

What kind of mammal has hair shaped like this? Turn the page to find out.

Useful words

caterpillar – the young stage of a butterfly or moth.

dolphin – a mammal that lives in the sea.

earthworm – a long thin animal with no legs.

egg – the first stage of animals.

fin – a part that sticks out from the body of a fish. It has long bones like needles.

gills – the part of a fish that lets it breathe underwater.

millipede - a long thin animal with a lot of legs.

magnifying glass – a piece of glass or plastic that makes small things look larger when you look through it.

moth – an insect which has two pairs of wings and flies about at night.

scales – small, flat, hard objects that cover the skin of fish and reptiles. They cover birds' legs too.

skin – a cover over an animal's body. Mammal skin grows hair. Fish and reptile skin grows scales. Bird skin grows feathers.

slug – an animal with a long, fat body, feelers at one end and no legs.

tadpole – the young stage of an amphibian when it looks like a fish.

woodlice – animals with lots of legs and a shell made up of many sections joined together.

28

Some answers

Here are some answers to the questions we have asked in this book. Don't worry if you had some different answers to ours; you may be right, too. Talk through your answers with other people and see if you can explain why they are right.

Page 7   This could be a very long answer! You could think of animals in groups like: pets, farm animals, wild animals.

Pages 10-11 A, B, D and H are insects. The millipede, earthworm, slug and woodlice are not insects. The millipede belongs to an animal group which also includes centipedes. The earthworm belongs to a worm group which includes leeches and lug worms. The slug belongs to the mollusc group which includes snails, and the woodlouse belongs to the crustacea group which includes shrimps and crabs.

Page 13   A and D are snails. B is a slug. C is an earthworm.

Page 23   Did you think of the birds you may see in a garden or a park like a sparrow, duck and swan? You could also think about powerful birds, such as an eagle and a hawk. Can you think of a bird that flies at night?

Page 27   The answers in the last column of the table should be, from top to bottom: **D** mouse, **A** slug, **B** fish, **C** beetle, **E** lizard, **F** bird.

Index

About this book

Ways into Science is designed to encourage children to begin to think about their everyday world in a scientific way, examining cause and effect through close observation, recording their results and discussing what they have seen. Here are some pointers to gain maximum use from **What Animal Is It?**

• Working through this book will introduce the basic concepts for identifying animals and also some of the language structures and vocabulary associated with them (for example fly, jump, run and comparatives such as tiny and huge). This will prepare the child for more formal work later in the school curriculum.

• On pages 9, 15, 19, 21 and 25 the children are invited to use their general knowledge about animals to predict the identity of a particular animal on the following page. Ensure that you discuss the reason for any answer they give in some depth before turning over the page.

• In answering the question on page 9 ask the children to compare the photograph with the information about insects on the spread. In answering the question on page 15 be prepared for unusual animals, such as the octopus. In answering the question on page 19 be prepared for an answer about crocodiles. These animals are reptiles but have an amphibious lifestyle. On page 21 the children may be surprised to find that a bird has got scales like a reptile. In answering the question on page 25 the children may be equally surprised to find that they are members of the mammal group.